Your Journey Goes On

25 Plus Years of Observations
by a Financial Advisor

Robert Cepeda, CFP®

Printed in the United States of America
First Printing 2019
First Edition 2019

10 9 8 7 6 5 4 3 2 1

Disclosures

Your Journey
Goes On

Acknowledgments

Over the years, through my own journey, I've come across many people who have influenced my life…family, friends, teachers, coaches, associates, and clients. All have contributed to my observations. I am most thankful to God. He has put all of the above on my path and has helped guide my continuing purpose.

TABLE OF CONTENTS

INTRODUCTION 1

PART ONE 9

    LIFE HAPPENS

CHAPTER ONE 11

    GETTING MARRIED

CHAPTER TWO 22

    HAVING CHILDREN

CHAPTER THREE 32

    DECIDING WHERE TO LIVE

PART TWO 36

    PLANNING FOR CHANGE

CHAPTER FOUR... 38

    JOB CHANGES

TABLE OF CONTENTS

CHAPTER FIVE 43

    COLLEGE

CHAPTER SIX 50

    PRE-RETIREMENT

PART THREE 68

    AND NOW WHAT?

CHAPTER SEVEN 70

    PARENTS

CHAPTER EIGHT 89

    LOSS OF SPOUSE

CHAPTER NINE 94

    THE JOURNEY GOES ON

AUTHOR BIO 98

INTRODUCTION

Dreams and Goals

I've found that people don't like to talk about their dreams and goals. Sometimes they have a thought, or an idea, but they think it is just a foolish dream. They're afraid to reach for it and say it out loud.

The truth is, if it stays in your head, then it will always be a dream. But if you put it on paper, make a plan, and have a person that will hold you accountable, you may accomplish more than you ever thought possible.

I'm that accountability person. I'm the coach.

Many people go to school to learn a trade or profession. Maybe, instead of school, they specialize in the workforce. In graduate school people learn how to be doctors, attorneys, teachers, etc. In short, we learn how to make money, but not how to handle it or invest it towards our dreams. The reason I'm in business is to coach you on your quest, and to the finish line.

I tell every client to start saving as much as possible, as soon as possible. I often relate it to physical training. You know you can do 30 pushups, but left alone, you're done. A good coach encourages you, "You can do more." So, you try. And, eventually, you can do much more than you thought possible.

It's the same with saving.

"I can't save that much," you say.

"Yes, you can. Just try it."

Eventually, saving becomes a pattern, a habit. My goal is to help my clients feel that they can accomplish more than they thought they could. I have sought to achieve more than I dreamed possible in my own journey.

My Journey

I grew up as an only child, but I was the last of ten kids. My parents had to work hard, and some of my siblings worked as well. One day, when I was just a year old, my mom had to leave me with a babysitter. The babysitter left me out on the patio, and when my mom came home, I was covered in bee stings. Obviously, no one had been watching me.

My aunt stepped in and offered to take care of me. I moved in with my aunt and uncle, who I call Mom and Dad.

One time they took me to visit my birth parents and tried to leave me. I asked them where they were going. When they said I was staying, I told them, unequivocally, that I was only staying for the weekend. I guess I knew that I didn't want to fight for food amongst all those siblings!

My family worked hard and earned good money but didn't save or even talk about saving and investing. No one talked to my family about financial planning. In college, I realized I wanted to have my own business. I had always been good at getting along with people and considered myself a strategist. What better field to study than financial planning! I could utilize my skills and training to help people pursue their financial goals and dreams.

After graduation, I started at a Wall Street-based company. While the home office was on Wall Street, I worked locally. When you work for a company, you learn that the company can take care of a person's needs with their products and services, but it may not be efficient. I worked there for a while, learned some specific skills and moved on.

I left the Wall Street firm to join an independent financial advisor, where I learned even more about the business. I started to crystallize how I would structure and run my own company. After four years, I broke away. My current partner and I founded Quest Financial Services in 1999.

My Business

The name of our company is Quest Financial Services because we are here to help you on your journey, your quest. When you go through the trials and tribulations of financial planning, you need someone alongside you to show you the way and protect you on your quest.

Not only do people want to know that they are financially sound until they pass, but they also want to know that the next generation will do even better financially.

As an independent company, we can work with any client, and we're free of the constraints of quotas and other practices that we don't like. At Quest, it is our belief that all recommendations should be in the best interest of our clients.

I lay out the possible outcomes as completely as I possibly can.

People will ask, "Can this fluctuate?"

I'll say, "Well, yes, it can."

"Is it guaranteed?" they want to know.

"No. It's not. But you have to have your parameters."

I'm always going to tell people the way it is. I'm their coach, and I want them to excel, that includes understanding the risks for any financial planning or investment strategy.

Why I wrote a book

The best part of being a financial advisor is seeing my clients achieve their life goals and hearing, "Thank you for getting me here." I hope that after reading this book, you will see that while everyone's situation is unique, the questions you may have are common across the board. Often it is intimidating to make decisions, but there is someone that you can rely on to help you make a plan.

This book divides into three sections. Each section has three chapters dealing with specific life stages. Over the years, I've lived through many life events, both difficult and joyful, with my clients. I've learned some lessons that will, hopefully, help you along your journey as they've helped me along mine.

In the age of specialization that we live in, people go to school to learn their craft and go to work to make money doing whatever it is that they do. But schools don't sit you down and say, "Okay, now that you're a doctor—let's talk about financials and what to do with your money."

They don't even give you real-world experience in things like balancing a checkbook—a hugely important skill and practice.

Very often, people are intimidated simply by the idea of a financial advisor. They don't know where to start, who to talk to, or even what questions to ask.

You don't need to worry about that.

The first time I meet with a new client, I'm just looking to get to know them and understand their goals. What is first and foremost on their mind? What do they want to address first?

Each person is a melting pot of goals and concerns that need to be addressed according to their finances. Are you worried about sending your children to college? Are you hoping to take a major vacation? Do you want to buy a boat, or maybe a house? Are you looking ahead to retirement?

Usually, people have one primary goal in mind, along with several smaller goals. Every stage of life brings additional trials and new goals that require planning.

People are conditioned to behave but not necessarily to dream. As a result, frequently, my first job is to help clients to articulate their dream or dreams.

I often tell the story about the flea experiment. Researchers put fleas into two different cups. The first cup was not covered; the fleas jumped out and escaped. The researchers placed a screen over the top of the second cup so the insects could not escape. The fleas jumped but were restrained by the screen.

The fleas in the second cup became conditioned to this limitation. Once conditioned, even after the screen was removed, the fleas did not attempt to escape. They continued to jump but only to the previous height of the screen.

The same is true of the human spirit. If you are told regularly that you can't do something, it becomes believable. However, if someone comes along and believes in you and says, "You can do this and here's the way to go about it," you can break down the mental barriers and conditioning. You have the encouragement to pursue your dreams and your quest. I'm the coach to encourage you towards your dreams.

I'm also there to tell you if your dream is unrealistic. You say you have two dollars saved and you want to travel the world? That's probably not going to happen this year, but let's make a plan for that dream.

Sometimes a new client will tell me, "I just want to save on taxes."

That's not a goal. That's a side effect of listening to your financial advisor as you work toward your goal.

Others tell me that their goal is to "make money." That is not a goal either. What is the money's purpose? Sometimes people accumulate wealth and have no use for it. There should be a purpose for what you're doing with your money.

People want to chase what has been done already. The next big thing has happened already, but they want to get in on it. It's too late to get in after it has already become popular.

If I get people to start thinking about what the future looks like and make it more concrete, then it's no longer arbitrary. You have a target at which to aim. Instead of just working to earn a paycheck and pay the bills, you have a goal. You have a quest.

I've always been big on writing down goals. When I write down my goals, they tend to happen sooner. I also learned in college that those individuals who were the most specific on their goals were most likely to achieve them, and to do it faster.

What am I going to do for you if you have no idea where you want to go? On your mark, get set, go! And you run, but when do you stop? How do you know if you've won if you don't see the location of the finish line? Without a finish line, you'll keep running until you pass out. That's not the way to win a race!

If you're doing a 400 meter race, you run as fast as you can around the track. If it's 800 meters, you run a little slower, twice around the track. For a marathon, you go slow and steady. If you don't know which race you're running, it's impossible to make a plan.

I believe it is essential for a client to write down their dream, make it a goal, and listen to coaching.

People are capable of much more than they think. I'm here to see where you stand, understand where you want to go, and show you the path that can lead you there.

PART ONE
LIFE HAPPENS

"We can make a plan, but a plan is as good as today because tomorrow you might be getting married, having kids or changing jobs."

CHAPTER ONE

Getting Married

"I'm not a therapist."

Your heart is pounding and you can't catch your breath. The world is a bright and glittering place where anything is possible. You've found your soulmate and you're about to live happily ever after.

That is, if you take a few steps to protect that happiness before you tie the knot.

Communication

Communication is the bedrock, the necessary foundation, for both a beautiful marriage and a healthy financial future. In my experience, very few couples have an honest conversation about their finances before they get married. This leaves most couples at a disadvantage and prone to surprises down the road. Talking about your finances, goals, and expectations is a necessary step when planning your future together— much more important than the wedding itself.

When I first meet with a new client, I want to know their goals. Before you get married, you need to discuss not *just* finances but your personal goals. If you're going to do one thing and your partner wants to do something else, and that is never actually communicated—the results can be disastrous.

The discussions about goals should cover everything from careers to homes, vacations to expensive cars, or especially the big-ticket items—children.

You can't necessarily plan when you're going to have kids, but the question of whether they are part of your anticipated future requires active consideration. If yes, how many do you plan to have? What happens when they are born? Are you going to stay at home? Will your spouse stay home? Will you get childcare?

The question you should be asking yourselves prior to marriage is, "Am I prepared to have only one income or can I handle the expense of childcare, in addition to the other hidden costs of my little dividend?"

Before you embark on this new life together, you should discuss obtaining insurance. You don't need to wait until you are married to obtain family protection. Get life insurance now, with the anticipation that you are going to be married long-term. After all, marriage isn't intended to be a seven-year contract with renewal. (That might be a good idea though!)

Right now, you know what your health issues are. And, you know you are going to need to protect your income for your surviving spouse and any children. No one knows when the unthinkable will happen, whether it is five years down the road or fifty. Get life insurance now while it's affordable. Lock it in.

Making a Budget

There's a certain amount of responsibility that you owe to each other when you get married. When it is just you, you only worry about yourself. When you have a team, you're responsible to each other and to that brand new person you may create.

Once you've established consistent and transparent communication and understand what the goals are for each person, you need to establish budgets and decide how all of your money is going to be spent—from expenses to discretionary spending to investments and retirement.

This is probably harder for the entrepreneur than the employee. I notice that a lot of teachers marry law enforcement. Those couples seem to be pretty stable. They work, save, and the financial stages of life arrive pretty much like clockwork. But, when you get other dynamics, like business cycles and income ebb and flow, it's different.

Perhaps you like to go to football games or concerts, but your future spouse would rather invest in their favorite hobby or compete in a Spartan race. You have to adjust for the fact that you each have different interests that are going to affect your budget. These are known as the discretionary items of your budget. Single people often forget to include these items in their individual budgets. But, spouses always notice their partners expenses!

A budget is generally comprised of three different types of expenses. There are the monthly expenses like rent and car payments that have to be paid if you don't want to ruin your credit. Then there are the things you need, but you can have some control over, like food, gas and your clothing. The cost of those items fluctuates depending on your tastes. Do you prefer high-end items or store brands? Then the last section—which no one counts and is the most fun—vacations, football games, concerts, gifts, going out to eat, and those types of things.

That last section is where the difficulty lies as a couple works out how they will budget for each other's "toys", hobbies, and interests. Couples need to honestly share their values and what they hold important. If your value systems are different, you are going to have conflict especially if you don't discuss those differences honestly. Unresolved conflict could lead one or both spouses to do things secretly. You should be able to do the things you love and discuss them openly with your spouse.

Financial success is based on communication. As a couple, you need to have shared clarity from the beginning. Shared clarity will lead to a shared understanding, and agreement on the budget.

The Wedding

Now it's time for the wedding. Who is going to pay for it? Is it going to be the parents or the young couple? In either case, no one should struggle to try to finance an event that will only last four hours.

People sometimes spend tens of thousands of dollars on weddings. The truth is, even if you've saved up for that expense until now, you're investing in something from which you will never see a return. You will never recoup what you put into a wedding, so there should be budgets and realistic expectations.

Today's generation needs to be creative. I'm hoping my kids get married in the backyard with a barbecue.

The financial reality is that the $10K-20K you spent on those four hours of bliss could be working much better for you thirty years from now in retirement. The trade-off could have ramifications on whether or not you work in your retirement, or what you can afford to do in your retirement.

I'm not trying to kill the romance or the magic of that special day. It's an event that some have fantasized about for years.

What I'm saying is that your family and your life are not a single day. Your love story does not end on the day of your wedding like the fairy tales. It's a fleeting moment in the epic adventure of your life together, and you need to plan accordingly, keeping focused on your long-term goals.

With the right financial plan, you could live happily ever after.

I'm not a Therapist

The number one reason for divorce is money. Only it's not. Not really. It's the failure to communicate about money. Add mismatched goals and expectations, and you're going to have trouble.

A while back I was speaking with a couple, and I could see there was much more going on under the surface. He was complaining about various things until finally, I had to interrupt him.

"Listen, I'm not a therapist, but I do have to tell you that I think you need to see someone to get through this. I'm not saying that to be mean or anything. But the reality is, you're both going to benefit from being able to communicate better. If you can't learn that skill, the real issues will fester and you will fight without really saying what's on your mind."

I'm not a therapist. I can't give any advice on individual interpersonal relationships, but sometimes I make the recommendation that a couple talk to a trained psychologist.

Too many marriages end because of the "finances." It's not actually the finances or even the bumps that every marriage endures along the way. The couple has never learned how to communicate about the bumps or, how to deal with difficulty together. Sometimes, it's uncomfortable to confront issues. However, it's better to reveal small misunderstandings or differences of opinion than to let those problems grow for years. When you harbor resentment, the only person that suffers is the person who harbors it. It's like holding a lump of red-hot coal in your bare hand. When you close your hand around it and squeeze it tighter and tighter all you are doing is scarring *your* hand. The other person has no idea anything is happening.

When you begin to communicate better, inevitably one spouse responds with surprise, "I didn't know you wanted to do that. I didn't know you wanted that from me."

Many times, I have met with a new client, and I could see that there was a particular marital issue because of money. Each time I had to explain that they needed to clear up the marriage issue before we could move forward with the financial matters.

I know it might not seem like financial planning, but a lot of psychology and therapy comes into play when it comes to people and their money!

People come into marriages a certain way, but often, they change over time. Sometimes, one spouse will try to create change, or manipulate the other person. Manipulation doesn't end well. In my experience, it is inadvisable.

Sometimes, if one personality is more dominant and their spouse doesn't say anything, only the dominant personality's goals will be accomplished. That can give rise to resentment and marital issues. But if the couple has good communication and conflict resolution skills, the goals of both can be achieved with compromise. That's really what a marriage is about.

I recall having a young couple come in. I was trying to help them formulate a plan. The husband had a business, but it was very draining. It was making a little money, but he wasn't managing it as well as he could.

What I realized, however, was that his business wasn't just a business to him. It was really about his empowerment or his self-worth.

His wife had asked him to get another job—a state job that would pay him well and provide a pension. It made all the sense in the world, but his resentment was overwhelming.

In his eyes, she was trying to take everything away from him. She was telling him to give up on something that had potential and that he loved.

Meanwhile, she thought she was being practical and trying to safeguard their financial future. She didn't realize the impact her request was having on him.

That's when I recommended a therapist. There were other issues and animosity, too. I knew this wasn't moving toward planning for retirement or being able to afford college. It was about their lives taking different paths, and that was going to be an altogether different issue.

After the professionals have been brought in to help a couple learn communication, we can begin a financial plan.

Sometimes, clients come in and admit that they feel as though they're locked in a battle over a particular financial decision. As we talk about it, we often find *not* that one is saying one thing and the other is saying something else—but they're saying the same thing from different perspectives.

For example, one person is focusing on buying a house in California, while the other is aiming for a home in Florida. They might both be warm places, but they're entirely different destinations.

The idea here is to get on the same page with your spouse from the beginning and visit a financial planner to come up with a roadmap for your shared dreams and goals.

Getting Married...Again

As I mentioned, financial disagreements often lead to dissolving the partnership. Perhaps one half wanted to put money toward retirement and resented spending money on something else. Regardless, there was disagreement and resentment that built until the relationship broke.

Now, lightning has struck twice, and you're considering a new merger.

It seems awful to talk about, but it's not outlandish to say, "Let's put an agreement in place first."

This request is usually the result of fear. I don't think there's anything wrong with having the discussion. Telling your future spouse, "I was married before and now that I'm getting married again, I want to make sure that my children are protected," is tough, but honest. Remember, communication is the foundation for success.

Sometimes the best way to get through conflicts of this nature is with a neutral mediator.

I had a divorced client who became engaged and was looking forward to her second marriage. Her future husband was very well off financially, and this was a second marriage for him, also. She didn't particularly care about how much he was making, but he was asking for a prenuptial agreement and the negotiations seemed unfair to her.

You can look at it from both sides. If something were to happen, the husband doesn't want to lose everything, especially if he already went through a messy divorce. On the other side of the coin, it is a marriage, and he should be protecting her as his wife.

All I'm saying is that the discussion should take place, and the conflicting points of view aired. Sometimes there are tough conversations when planning to merge two different lives, and I can't tell you which are the right and wrong answers. The dynamics are going to be different for every situation. I can't say what the right answer is for your situation.

Hopefully, we've learned from the previous experience, and we're communicating from day one, without being afraid to ask the tough questions.

Happily Ever After

On the other side of the spectrum, there are couples that come in and tell me as a team that they have the same goals, and they know what they want.

The most important thing to remember when you are getting married is to make sure everyone is on the same page. The chapters of your life together will flow more easily toward that happily ever after.

CHAPTER TWO

HAVING CHILDREN

"Children are great, but they can be expensive."

Once children are born, there are several new areas of life that require consideration. People will come to me and say they want to do something for the kids to make sure the kids have additional provision later in life. Often, what they want to do, what might seem logical to do, is the last thing they should do.

Insurance

I have had clients that purchased life insurance on their kids, in case the unthinkable happened. The issue here is that you're putting money toward something that you shouldn't. Life insurance is about financial loss. One of the worst things to happen at any age is for a child to predecease their parents. But if a young child passes away, there is no financial loss.

If a child passes away, yes, it is excruciating, but you only have to take on the cost of the funeral. Whereas, if you die, the remaining family has to take on bills that will continue to arrive. If those bills aren't planned for, and, no financial provision is made for your children, they will become a burden on someone else. Of course, another person is going to love your child. But providing for on-going living expenses and college education funding helps reduce the stress and makes a horrible tragedy easier for all involved.

Don't worry about insuring the children—make sure *you're* insured. That way, if something happens to you, the children have adequate provision and the best opportunity to thrive.

Sometimes out of the best of intentions, we end up doing things backward. We love our kids and want to protect and provide for them—but to do that, we need to take care of ourselves first. The reality is, if a parent were to pass away or get hurt, the money needs to keep flowing.

Prepare a Will

I am not an attorney, and so please do not misconstrue this as legal advice. I have come across so many people that say they never made a will. It is a tool that works in conjunction with correct financial planning, especially when you have children. If you don't have a will, the state is going to dictate who is going to take care of the children. Or, you can have family members fighting over who will, or won't, take care of the children.

The will is part of good communication, letting all of the interested parties know the plan. Don't wait and ask that relative, that friend, before you get on the plane for a vacation or work trip, "Just in case, our plane goes down we had this drawn up to protect our children and us—would you be willing to care for our children?"

Without a will specifying who is going to care for the children, you have the government getting involved and the sister arguing with the in-law's grandparents. It happens.

Many parents think about these things at the last second, sitting at the airport. "We don't have any paper, so we're going to write on the back of this receipt, sign it and give it to our parents. I think it might hold up in court."

You want to have something more legally binding and well-considered. It shouldn't be a last-minute scramble on the eve of a trip. That approach opens the door to errors, overlooked situations, and concerns about whether it will pass muster in court.

Major Vacations

I always find it interesting when people take major vacations with children. When you take your one-year-old to Disney, a significant vacation, who is the vacation really for? It wasn't for the kid. I'm going to make a bet that your child is not going to remember what they did on this vacation ten years from now. They won't even know that they went to Disney!

About ten years ago, my mother told me she took me to Disney when I was one or two years old. I have absolutely no recollection of that.

"What? No, you didn't! Why are there no pictures? Why have you never mentioned this before?" I demanded.

When I confronted my father, he said the same thing.

"Are you sure? Did she tell you to say that?"

I still don't believe it to this day. The reality is, if they did take me, I don't remember.

My wife was itching from the day our first child was born to take her to Disney World (or maybe it was me!). I had to break the news gently.

"She's two years old, and you're pregnant—we're not going to Disney World...yet"

Later, we were fortunate in that my parents moved to the state of Florida so we would visit them and yes, go to Disney World. We were careful to make it cost-effective, staying with them and going in the offseason. It's all about planning. This approach worked well until my oldest was in the sixth grade, and missing school started to be more of an issue. It became too hard to help her catch up!

Kids don't need expensive vacations to make lasting memories.

I remember when my youngest daughter, I think she was four or five years old, said, "When are we going to the hotel and stay at the pool?"

I'll do that trip any time, and my kids are going to remember that as being as memorable as going to Disney or flying off to California or something else. Just keep things simple. You don't need to go overboard. Consider who is dictating what you are doing and the success of your budget. Sometimes, it is the kids.

If you want to take that major vacation with the children when they're old enough, that can be a goal. If you want to get to the point financially where you can take a nice vacation every year, that can be a goal. What I recommend is to take care of your expenses and skip a year or two until your budget and your savings are sound. When you do take that vacation, you want to be able to relax by the pool or beach without having to worry about how you're going to pay for it.

I remember speaking to a client and asking how they had built up a lot of credit card debt. They explained, "Well, we took this trip and had to put it on a credit card. We're still paying it down, but you know what, it was so memorable!"

I can see if you're doing it as a one-time thing. But if you're looking to go on a specific adventure, it can be planned out.

I'm not saying you have to live on bread and water. But there are certain limits, and you need to keep it to a reasonable expectation. If you're coming to me and you're carrying this debt—credit card debt which is the worst kind of debt—that means you probably did something that you shouldn't have done, or you didn't have an emergency fund built up to protect yourself.

A credit card at the beginning of adult life is your emergency fund. With an emergency fund, you have money to the side so if you need it, you use it, but you replenish it quickly. A credit card is the same way. If you need it and you don't have an emergency fund, then you use it, but you pay it off quickly. It's an inefficient form, but life does happen, and sometimes things are out of our control.

I would prefer that people didn't use a credit card. If they're using a credit card and have accumulated a lot of credit card debt, I find that there's frequently a timeshare that they've visited once or never. They visited a timeshare when their kids were young, but they don't remember the trip, and they're never going to visit again. It's the craziest thing.

Look at the balance. What are you giving up taking an expensive vacation? It's just like any other type of coaching. We can do this, but what are you giving up for it?

When a vacation is a goal, sometimes people try to fulfill it early by taking on debt. And once accomplished, the debt doesn't go away. The parents want to do it again, and the children don't remember it.

Instead, what I try to tell people is to create the habit. Don't go on vacation this year, take care of some things, and skip a year, which is ok. You're still young. Plan it out so then it's within your budget, and later, next year, or two years from now, you can take that bigger vacation.

Now you can go on vacation every year—because we've planned it out. It's all part of your budget, and you're also taking care of your retirement. That's important, too. Do you want to continue taking vacations when you retire? Well, if you're not putting the money away now, you're not going to be able to do that.

Unnecessary Spending

Think about the gifts you give during the holidays. Once the gifts are unwrapped, how memorable was it? Now, I know, I did it too. I will do as much as I can for my kids, within my budget, but there are certain things we all have to realize. Our children can't play with fifteen gifts at once and building up debt for those presents isn't helping matters.

We tend to go to great lengths to do as much as we can for our children. I'm not saying this is right or wrong, but you don't necessarily need to send your kids to private school.

You say you want to send your kids to a private school because you've heard that students don't do as well in your local school. However, I will tell you that if you're doing it to avoid bullying and the like, it won't work.

I went through the public-school system, so I'm big on just going to the public schools. If a bully is sitting next to you at that private school, it's just as bad as a bully at the public school. I don't think there's any escaping that. So now you're paying for the greatest school with a jerk child next to your kid.

What I'm saying is that we want to do everything we can for our children. But, we have to be careful and mitigate how our children are running our lives.

If you can't afford certain things, you have to understand that there's a trade-off. You don't want to explain to your children that you spent their college fund on private schools.

My recommendation to my clients is that they should have their child come in and talk to me at a young age. The best thing I can have them do is make sure they are putting money away for themselves now.

I say that only for the simple fact that if I get that child to put away money now, and not say, ten years from now, or twenty years from now, then they will have a good start. If I can get them to understand the philosophy of how money works, then they're not coming in to visit me with a substantial debt later, saying, "I wish I had talked to you sooner."

The fact is, as time goes on, our children don't get less expensive. Today's generation is living at home into adulthood.

One solution: charge your kids rent.

Now, I'm not saying to start when they're in elementary school. When your fledgling is at the point of either seeking higher education or entering the workforce, they should also take on the responsibility of their room and board. It will encourage them to fly the nest, or at the very least, offset the expenses they incur and teach them responsibility. They need to understand that there is a cost to everything.

It is up to you if you want to apply that income to your expenses or put it away for your child for the large expenses life will inevitably bring their way: a vehicle, college, or even a wedding. Just don't let them know until you're ready to hand over their surprise savings account.

Then, after they've started their adult life...they have children of their own. Grandchildren can be just as expensive.

Often, I will have clients come in, and we have to make some tough decisions. Before they walked in, they didn't plan well, so now they find themselves in the unenviable position of trying to make their money last.

"I see this line item is gifts. You spend quite a bit."

"Oh, they're for the grandchildren."

"You have to be careful about what you spend. Your grandchildren understand that you can't spend the same that you did before."

It's a tough conversation at times. I explain that their children and grandchildren would rather that they continue to live the same lifestyle, without debt, than spend their entire legacy. Grandma and Grandpa don't want to spend so much money on gifts that they have to move in with their children!

In your retirement, I know you would love to spoil your grandchildren, and you can, within your budget.

Just remember that children—and grandchildren—are great, but they can be expensive.

CHAPTER THREE

Deciding where to live

> *"If you want the mansion on the hill, but you're saving for the shack in the valley, I'll tell you."*

Deciding where to live can have a profound effect on not just your life, but also your finances.

Location, location, location

It's funny that after your parents pass, you learn what they did for you.

When I went to live with my mom and dad (aunt and uncle), we lived in the Bronx until after I completed kindergarten. Then we moved to Middletown, New York, which is closer to Ellenville, New York, where the rest of the family lived. From there, I went to Goshen, New York schools starting in fourth grade.

During those years, my father (uncle), tried to get jobs locally, but he couldn't get the same pay grade. He commuted to New York City for work. I decided that I didn't want to do the same. It was grueling for him to travel for two hours each way every day. Sometimes he'd be out the whole week, and I'd only see him on the weekends. It was a struggle.

I didn't understand why he was doing it, but I just knew I didn't want to have the same lifestyle. It wasn't until recently that I found out why we moved.

When I was a few years older, my mom had asked that my aunt bring me back. My aunt she said she couldn't.

"I'll die if you take him," my aunt said.

My mother told my father, "I don't want my sister to die."

So, my mom agreed that I could stay with them longer, but only if we lived closer to Ellenville. So, we moved to Middletown.

I always knew he loved me very much, but it didn't hit me until much later on that he had to commute to the city so that he could maintain his job and the family could stay close to Ellenville.

I learned that people of modest means can do great things. He paid for my braces, and I was able to attend the University of Rochester—which I feel is a great school.

The situation for others may be different, but there is always a sacrifice deciding where to live. It all depends on what is most important to you. Some people don't want to commute to New York City, so they'll live in Manhattan. Well, how much is that going to cost? Is it something you can afford on your salary?

Buying a Home

It's the same concept when considering purchasing a home. Are you looking for a large, modern home? Will the cost be something you can absorb, or will you find yourself swimming in debt? That is what is called being house poor.

Everybody wants to live like the Jones'. They want to live in that big house and drive an expensive car. Sometimes the better thing is not to live like the Jones' now. Wasting money now on large consumable items can result in suffering down the road.

Early on in my career, I was approached by a married couple that wanted to figure out their finances and buy a home. Based on the way they were spending, I had to give them the hard truth.

"Based on what you have going on and how much you would have to put down, you're not going to be able to buy a house."

I think they were a little upset with that! A couple of years later, I was talking to them, and they said, "Oh, just to let you know, we got that house."

"That's great!"

"Yeah, you said we couldn't get it."

My point wasn't that they couldn't purchase a house. My point was that based on what they needed to have put away and the savings they had disclosed to me, combined with their current spending habits, it was an inopportune time to pursue it. I guess, instead, I gave them a challenge. I think they may have gotten a sub-prime mortgage.

When I was a brand-new financial advisor I lived in a one-room apartment. I had an old car that I drove to my first appointment. It was winter, and I needed a blanket in my car because the heat wouldn't work. It was embarrassing at the time, but I had to deal with what I could afford and keep my own financial goals and plans in mind. I could have spent money getting the car fixed or on a new car, but waiting just a little longer was more responsible.

Today, it seems like the trend among the younger generation is not to buy a home at all.

Instead, they are moving to a less permanent living situation, with barely any commute, have jobs that didn't exist a few years ago, and only visit the office once or twice a week.

It's fantastic, and it seems like that is the direction our society is heading. Soon, being in a state like New York will not be as crucial as it was in the past.

PART TWO

Planning for Change

CHAPTER FOUR

Job Changes

The focus of your financial planning should be your retirement. Life happens, and sometimes, you can lose a job or become disabled (which is almost like losing a job).

Protect the Money Machine

You have to think about what will happen if you lose your employment or have to take a different job at a lower pay rate. It will be a struggle, but this is when you support each other.

Whenever there is a job change, we have to make sure, like when you got married, that you're protecting the money machine.

Here's the question that I ask my clients: If you had a machine that created $1,000 a week sitting in your garage, would you insure it?

Of course! And how is it any different from insuring a person who can become disabled and no longer able to work? Or die, for that matter? You need to make sure that person is protected. If a breadwinner dies, their income is gone, so you have to make sure there's life insurance. You have to make sure you're protecting the family.

I had one client that didn't want to get life insurance. I told him that he needed to protect the money machine and his family. Finally, with a little grumbling, he applied for life insurance. With the required blood testing, they found out that he had diabetes. He thanked me profusely, saying that he could have died if I hadn't pushed him. He got his diet under control, and his diabetes receded.

I reminded him that he still needed to get life insurance. This time he was more amenable. That is, until they told him that it was going to be more expensive than usual because of the diabetes diagnosis.

"I'm not going to do it!"

"What do you mean, you're not going to do it? The insurance is for your family. You've got to do this."

He finally agreed, and we ended up getting coverage for about $1.2 million.

A while later, I called, but I couldn't get in touch with him. Then, he canceled our next scheduled appointment. While out at the store during the holiday season, I bumped into him and asked how he was doing.

"I'm sorry about that. I was recently diagnosed with stomach cancer."

He told me he was doing fine and receiving treatment. I remember going to his house, and he was on the couch. He didn't look good at all, and I asked how he was feeling.

"I'm dying of cancer."

His delivery was both funny and tragically accurate. He was a therapist and good at talking about the hard things. I was glad to see him and to say our goodbyes. I've done a number of those visits since then, where I left a client knowing that I had probably seen them for the last time.

Later, we scheduled another appointment, which he canceled. This time, I had a bad feeling about it. A few months later, he died. His cancer had progressed.

If you have cancer, you can't get life insurance. While the passing of my client was tragic, he put his life insurance coverage in place when he still could. As a result, he said he was able to live longer and protect his family when he passed.

You don't know what will happen. That's what planning is all about. You plan for the unexpected because anything can happen. Dementia. Diabetes. Cancer. They're affecting 100 percent of the population. Everyone knows someone or is related to someone who has cancer.

It's not that it's going to happen to you, but you need to plan and protect the money machine. It's about the "just-in-case."

Create the Habit

You also need to create a habit of saving. It's important to be able to put away money for the future. Everything needs balance, including making sure you're not trying to do too much or taking on unnecessary debt.

The reason you make plans and make sure you have money set aside is that you want to fill the gap between losing one job and finding another.

The toughest change would be losing a job in a metropolitan area like New York City, where you could be making $150,000 each year, and taking a new job in a less urban area where the best offer is $50,000.

And that happens. It happened to one of my clients.

My client was living locally here in Orange County and working at Citibank in New York City. He was laid off and started looking for a job closer to home. Now the differential is, if he worked in the city and lived in the city, it would have been more expensive. Because he lived here in the suburbs, he was able to maintain his lifestyle longer as he conducted his job search. If he had lived in an expensive apartment in the city, he would have felt the effects of the job loss more immediately.

Today, more people are losing their jobs or changing jobs, and usually more than once in their lifetime. You want to make sure that emergency funds are protecting you for about three months. An emergency fund will bridge your gap, and a disability insurance will pay if you are disabled. Life insurance will help your family should the catastrophic occur.

I always warn my clients to be wary of something called the wealth effect. Essentially, the wealth effect says that the more money we make, the more we tend to live into that lifestyle.

If instead, we can control ourselves early on so that as we get raises or bonuses, we take a large chunk of that and put it into our retirement plans or toward an emergency fund, it will be there for us when we need it.

Let's say you started a new job a few years ago, making $100,000. Over the years, you received raises, and you find yourself making $150,000. Suddenly, the company downsizes, and the only job you can find is offering $100,000. If you were saving those raises over the years and you're conditioned to live on $100,000, you can live with that job change for some time.

Often when I talk to a client's child that is beginning their career, I encourage them to live on less right from the beginning.

"So, you've got your first job-congratulations! I understand they're paying you $100,000. Now, say they gave you the job, but they can only pay you $85,000. Are you going to turn down that job?"

More often than not, they say, "No, I'll take that job."

"So then take that fifteen percent and put it away. Start yourself off early, and as you go along, you'll get to a certain point where you're saving more."

What you are doing is maximizing. If you maximize what you're putting into your retirement plans early on, you may have the potential to dictate when you want to retire. It's a matter of how aggressive you're going to be now.

When you change jobs, consider what you want to do with the 401K from your previous employer. From an investment standpoint, people shouldn't just let their money linger. Often, a better place to put your money is your own personal IRA to have more control and more freedom of choice than just leaving it at your last employer's 401k. While they did it as a benefit, the benefit loses its luster when you're gone.

It's important to address that account and reassess your financial planning when there's a change in jobs, for better or worse. Sometimes we take a better job, sometimes we take a different kind of job, sometimes we take a lower-paying job, but they all affect your future goals.

CHAPTER FIVE

College

"Sometimes there are tough conversations in financial planning."

One of the worst things to do is worry about your children without worrying about yourself first.

I know, that feels wrong, but it's not. You have to take care of yourself first. A wedding is a four-hour event, college is a four-year event, but retirement is the rest of your life. We don't put enough emphasis on those relationships (4-hours, 4-years, rest-of-your-life).

If you decide to pay for the college tuition of your children and after those four years, everything you've put away is gone, you can't retire because you don't have anything. Instead, your children have to help you, and you become a burden. You want to make sure that you don't become a burden. You want to make sure the next generation is better off than your generation.

If you, instead, consistently save into a retirement plan, you may have a significant amount put away by the time your children are ready for college. At that time, we can freeze what you're doing, and instead of putting the money toward retirement, that amount goes toward college. Meanwhile, your retirement still quietly grows.

When people see that they are saving so much money and so much taxes, they don't want to stop! They find a way to keep saving and pay for college. That's the way it works. It's living within your means. It's funny how that works.

One client that I worked with had the goal to maximize what they were saving, so they were living on less. They would joke about how they couldn't spend a lot of money, but then college came around.

They decided, ok, we're going to pay for college, and we're going to pay it out of pocket, so we're going to lower what we're paying toward retirement. Then, while they were able to pay for college, they noticed that their taxes had increased. Immediately, they went to go back to putting money toward retirement. They still found a way to pay college. I've seen it time and time again.

Those experiences are why I say: I'm going to trick you into saving. Because this is the way you're going to get through every stage of life.

A lot of times people don't think about the fact that college is negotiable. The value system should be, what we should try to encourage, is that just because you want to get into a specific school doesn't mean that's the school you should attend.

Be Realistic

The child's expectations have to be realistic. If we only make this much, we can afford to give you this amount. Even if you're smart enough to get into a good school—an expensive school—financially, it doesn't work.

One couple asked me if I could help them figure out how to pay for their son's college tuition. He was accepted to a great school, and he wanted to go. It was going to cost $30,000.

"Ok, so how much are you going to contribute to that?"

"Well,...nothing."

At this point, I was confused and confessed that I wasn't sure what they wanted me to say.

"Well, he got accepted, and he wants to go to this school, but we can't afford any of this, so we don't know if there's anything that can be done."

Sometimes, there are tough conversations in financial planning.

"The planning for that should have happened a while ago," I had to explain. One of the toughest things you're going to have to say to your son is 'you can't go.' Try a different school.

The parents couldn't afford the cost of the college, and that was the reality. They were looking at having their son take on more debt to go to the school he wanted. Unfortunately, this usually comes back to bite people later on.

Sometimes parents have to make a decision for a child or help them out, but they're not necessarily going to make the right decision.

I had another client ask me to help their child.

"She has these student loans and she's having a tough time affording them. We want you to see what you can do."

"How much are the student loans?"

"$150,000."

"How much does she make?"

"She makes $40,000. She's a social worker."

I'm not sure if you can understand what it is like to look someone in the eye, and say, there's not a whole lot to do. I can't help her. I don't even know what to say. This is why it is important to make plans for the future.

Now I could steer her toward finding a not-for-profit position, with the hope of having her loans forgiven as time goes on. But that's not planning. The planning should have been a conversation with her parents before college, explaining that they understood she liked a certain school, but they couldn't afford it and to choose an alternative.

It's one of the toughest things, to tell our children no. But we can't let the kids dictate what we do—especially if we can't afford it. If a child wants a car, you buy something in your price range, even if they beg for a Mercedes.

It's the same thing with college. Be realistic about the expectations. It's good for your kids to aim high or try for better, but you need to make sure that you're not putting them in a bad position.

That was a tough situation. The daughter that had become a social worker took on an extra job. I was honest with her that she was in a tough spot and I tried to coach her to start looking and thinking outside the box if she was going to make it—to try starting a regular group therapy session where she could charge per person.

And that's really all that you can say to pay that much debt. There are literally no other options. How else can you make yourself marketable?

But I'm not a business builder—I'm just someone who can look in from the outside, help manage the monies, and give guidance.

It is important to look at your situation, like that other college student. I believe he was a smart child, and in the end, he garnered a few scholarships, more aid, and he worked his butt off to go to the college he wanted. Even so, his parents were going to assist with something like $5,000 a year.

Skin in the Game

When I meet with a client early on, I share certain philosophies. For instance, that it's laudable that as parents, they want to be able to pay for their child's college tuition, but I want my children to pay a portion. I think it's important that they have some skin in the game and understand how hard it is to pay for college.

My daughter was choosing between two different schools. She loved one, but the second one had a better package, so we visited the campus. She loved it.

I said, "Look, we can visit your first-choice next week, but we already know they're not going to give you any more. They came down as far as they can. I can argue with them to try and get it down more, but if you love this school, why are we going to make this decision tougher?"

She decided to go to her second choice.

In the beginning, she had twinges of regret of how it might have been different at the first school, but she's now in her third year and loves her school.

When your children want something badly, ask them, "What are you going to do to work for it?"

When my daughter was in kindergarten, I planted the seed.

"Listen, honey, you may not understand this now, but if you get a full scholarship to college, I'm going to get you a brand-new car."

As she got older, I kept reminding her of that story. Now in eighth grade, she start to get really familiar with things. She was on the honor roll and getting good grades.

"I'm so proud of you!" I told her. "Now, remember, I said if you get a full scholarship--"

"Yeah, Dad, about that car...I was thinking about a Lamborghini."

"I said a new one; I didn't say which new one!"

Later in high school, she was applying for different scholarships, and I'm reminding her to try and get scholarships from wherever she can because I'll get her a new car (not a Lamborghini) if she gets a full scholarship. Afterward, she pauses and looks at me.

"Uh, Dad, do you know how hard it is to get scholarships?"

Of course, I told her I would still work something out with her if she could get partial scholarships. It's good to give incentives. I could have paid her tuition for college, but I believe that our children should have some skin in the game.

I'm not saying that you shouldn't help your children go to college. What I'm saying is that you should do what you can afford.

Some people are very proud of putting their children first financially.

"I have a lot of money put away for my son and daughter."

"How much did you put away for yourself?"

"Well none, I want to make sure that they're in a better position than me."

The fact is, you can pay for your child's college for four years, but without putting money away for your retirement, you could become a burden to your child.

As you start planning for retirement, you have to start living on less now, because you are not going to have enough money if you don't do anything now for retirement.

CHAPTER SIX

Pre-Retirement

"I'm going to trick you into saving."

You don't plan for retirement when you're just about to retire. At least, not if you actually want to retire! Unfortunately, that's what many people tend to do—they walk in to talk to a financial advisor, looking to retire.

Sometimes people want to do financial planning when it's too late. They should be talking to a financial advisor well before that, to create the plan. What does that retirement look like and what steps do we need to take to get there? When people start to look at the numbers and realize that they may not have been saving what they might need for retirement, they should begin to do so, and not continue to delay saving.

Sometimes there are hard truths to accept. We may not be able to do everything to the extent that you want to do it. You have to be realistic about what your goals are and about what you're trying to accomplish.

The question everyone seems to ask is: "How are we doing compared to other people?"

The answer is that it depends on your situation and not necessarily how much you make. Some people may make a much higher salary than you, and they can't retire. But because you're a spendthrift, you can do it. There are also ways we can go about doing it, that, depending on your situation, will help make your money last longer.

If you plan early, you increase your potential to live the retirement you want to live and be able to pass along something to your heirs. I think that's super important.

Where will you retire?

When I talk to clients about pre-retirement, I try to get them to start thinking about where they want to live when they retire. They shouldn't be waiting to figure that out until the year before they retire. That can be done years in advance.

One client came in and told me that he and his wife wanted to sell their New York home and buy a house in South Carolina when they retired. I asked them what they were waiting for, which surprised them. I explained that they could borrow off the house they owned locally. Then, with a line of credit ready, they could shop for, and purchase the home they wanted in South Carolina.

They were making good money and could afford to pay a mortgage once again. They followed my advice and purchased the home they wanted. After working a few more years, they retired, sold their home in New York and paid off the South Carolina mortgage. Now they have the place in South Carolina that they wanted, and it has appreciated because the real estate market went up.

This story shows the importance of planning. What could have happened was that the couple could have walked in and told me that they were retiring the following year. We would have had to scramble, and they would have been trying to sell the house only to then begin their search for a home in South Carolina. It would have been a reactionary approach.

Instead, it was a very calm transition. The most stressful thing the couple encountered was getting the movers to move their belongings. Unlike many people, they weren't worrying and hoping they could close on both houses at the same time. They sold the New York house and paid off the South Carolina house, done.

The process was purposeful; the way planning is supposed to happen.

My father (my uncle) has a similar story. He had it in his head to go to Florida when he retired—he wanted warm weather. At age 62, he said he was done and moved. My parents sold the house to me, took all of their belongings, and headed off to the Sunshine State. It happened so quickly that I was left sitting in the empty house with just my bedroom set and a small television, wondering what had just happened!

I have always loved what he did. He had that goal for himself and went for it. He hadn't done a lot for his retirement, but he didn't spend a lot either. That's so important when we're talking about retirement.

My parents bought a place in Florida and mowed the lawn for a few years before they decided to have someone come and do it. Otherwise, they didn't have many other expenses to worry about. They didn't travel, but they didn't want to either. They enjoyed their quiet life at home. Once in a while, they would go up the road to a Spanish restaurant for a nice evening. It was that simple, and they loved it. They did it, and they weren't expecting anything more.

My father was happy. He was able to live his dream. Yes, he passed away having problems at the end, but he had ten years living his dream retirement before dementia began to steal him away. Our family had many great trips visiting him down there.

I have always loved that he never let anybody impose their goals on him. He just enjoyed his life.

Your retirement is more than just where you want to live. It's also what do you want to do? What do you want your retirement lifestyle to be?

What is your goal?

I have some clients who may not have a lot of money, but they also don't have the desire to do a lot of things. They may want to retire to a small house in the backwoods of South Carolina. They buy the house for about $50,000, have no taxes, cook at home, and it's perfect for them. They don't need much. They have their TV and hobbies, and they're happy.

On the other hand, I also have clients who want to travel, experience new things, and dine out. That costs money, and you have to account for those expenses in your retirement planning.

I've said it a few times: if it's a dream that you want, write it down. Now it's a goal.

Sometimes, people get caught up in their minds about what they can accomplish. We live in a society that tells us, "You can't do this, you can't do that, that's never going to happen, or how are you going to manage that?" I'll tell you, "Fight for your dreams."

If you don't talk to somebody about your dream, and then go through the process to deconstruct it and figure out how to make it happen, it won't happen. If there's no plan, it's just luck, and luck really doesn't happen that often. But when you plan, then you can say, "Well, I like the warmer weather, so what does it take to be able to retire somewhere warm?" Let's do the research. What does it take to have that?

Universally, the answer is to start saving early on.

Making the Dream a Reality

Once we know the goal, we can work out a plan. The more information you give me, the better the plan is going to be. I can look at your finances, determine how much income you need for retirement, and backtrack it to create a plan—a plan that entails saving what you have now so you can enjoy it in your retirement.

People often say, "I don't really want to do that, but I see your point."

Everything you tell me is just another piece to the puzzle until finally we can see the whole picture and develop a plan.

Now, if you leave things out, then the plan doesn't work. For instance, if you forget to tell me about that timeshare you can't seem to sell, we may not end up with the results you expected!

I often explain that financial planning is like crossing the Atlantic Ocean. In the middle, it's easy to navigate, you're putting money away. It's harder to make mistakes when you have a lot more time. And, you can take a slightly longer route if you see a storm coming.

Once you near that shore of retirement, however, you need someone to guide you into the right decisions. You don't use the same type of investments at that point; the plan gets a little more specific. I've been told that when ships come into an unfamiliar port, someone comes from the land side and *they* steer the boat to the dock because they can navigate past the hazards more adeptly. It's the same thing.

In your twenties, you should come in to start your financial planning. You think you're ok, then you walk into a financial advisor's office, and he asks a question you never considered. That's because you're not trained to think about every question and a financial planner is.

Diversify

One of the ways to protect your retirement is to avoid putting all of your money into one investment. If it's doing well, that's great. Your assets are attached to a hot air balloon, heading for beautiful blue skies. But if something happens to that one balloon, all of your assets are now attached to an anvil that's heading for rock bottom.

For example, I tell my clients that if you're going to have a rental property, don't go after a single house or a single tenant because you have too much risk. If you're going to buy a rental property, pursue a complex where there are five buildings. In this scenario, if you lose a tenant, you don't lose your entire income from the property.

Put another way, say you own a pizzeria and lease space at a strip mall. You make some money, and you decide to invest...in another pizzeria. Now an issue comes up. That could be anything from the economy as a whole, or something environmental that affects the dairy industry. If everything you have is dedicated to the one investment, you're simply sinking. You have to plan to protect yourself from a disaster.

You could take out insurance on your business. But are you protected if something happens to you? What if something happens to the storefront? Anything can happen. You still need to have other assets.

When it comes time for financial independence (retirement), buyers may not line up and say, "You're selling this business? Great! Let me buy it." You need additional assets as a hedge of protection.

You might want to cash out, but it could be more difficult than you anticipate. You should be saving money, also.

By age 35, if not sooner, you need to be saving for your goal of financial independence. If at that age you're not really sure when you want to retire, or at least begin considering what retirement means or what you want your lifestyle to be, it may not happen.

Financial and retirement planning have to be purposeful. With the caveat that it's ok to change your mind along the way.

Things Change

In every stage, you do financial planning again. The first time I sit down with somebody, I do a financial plan. I repeat the process a few years later, because of lifestyle changes. We need to do it again because what you may have thought back in your early thirties is different than what you are doing in your fifties and maybe even your sixties. So, let's take a look at it like you're meeting me for the first time. Yes, I know your information, but, I'm more or less going to be digging for the heart of the matter—what is your goal? —because your values may have changed.

It's ok to change your values and goals.

Sometimes, people feel like they can't change their goals, as though they're letting someone down.

I thought I was going to be a dentist. Before I realized that my dream was financial planning, I told everyone I was going to be a dentist. When people bump into me from high school, they invariably ask, "I thought you were going to be a dentist? Why aren't you a dentist?"

I was going to college, and I read the statistics. At the time, dentists had the highest suicide and divorce rates. Today that has changed, but it gave me pause and the opportunity to discover my true passion. Regardless that I had been telling people for years that I was going to be a dentist, I pursued my goal of financial planning, and it has made all the difference.

The truth is, you may discover that you hate your old dream. Everyone dreams of a vacation or retirement at the beach. I took a beach trip once, and I found it sandy and sweaty. I hated it. Some people thrive on that, but I didn't. What if I had been planning to buy a home on a beach somewhere when I retired? What if I never checked out the beach to discover that I don't like it?

Sometimes people think they want something until they experience it. Then they realize it doesn't live up to the image they had in their minds.

Go out and do things that are outside of your comfort zone. Try the things that you are dreaming of doing in your retirement. On your next planned vacation, do a trial retirement. You may discover that you hate the beach, you don't like a Southern climate, or you get miserably seasick.

One of my clients told me she was thinking about selling her home, getting a camper, and driving around the country in her retirement. Well, she tried it.

"This sucks," she told me.

"So, it went well?"

"I have to travel all the time. I don't know people. I don't really want to drive. I thought this was my goal, but…it's not."

Life happens, and just as circumstances change, so do people and their goals. You always have the power of choice.

The path to the goal, however, always means putting money away for the long-term. I remember when I was young, and I wanted a house with lots of property. I learned quickly that I don't like mowing the lawn and I don't mind having neighbors nearby.

I advise my clients to put the money away and not to focus on the returns. I always bring up the story of Rip Van Winkle. He looks at his account statement in 2008 and says, "Oh, that looks pretty good." He goes to sleep and wakes up in 2018, looks at it again and laughs, "Wow, that's awesome!"

But the people that stayed awake in 2009 saw the market go down from a maximum value down to 50 percent of it and they panicked. Some people got out of the market, and their money never recovered. You need to put it there, forget about it, and know what the long-term plan is because you're not really putting it away for tomorrow.

Your emergency fund is what you use for concerns you might have for tomorrow. If you need that money for tomorrow, you may not want it tied to the market. I have regular meetings with clients so that if something changes, if they say they need money next week or next year, then we plan to carve some of that out because they don't want to take a risk on it. We want to make sure that their money is there for them when they need it.

Rip Van Winkle didn't worry about it. He didn't lose any sleep. He didn't pay any attention to it. But the people that watch regularly, they're the ones who need consistent financial guidance.

"Hey, remember what we talked about?"

I'm the coach. I remind them of their goal, of how much they wanted to set aside for retirement, the fact that sometimes the market will go up and sometimes it'll go down, and not allow emotions to guide your decisions.

Back in 2008, there were people in the news saying, "Oh my gosh, I was going to retire next year, but we lost so much money in the market!"

In my mind, if they were going to retire next year, why didn't they have money set aside to protect that short-term? We can't predict what the market is going to do. The maxim goes that if you need money short-term, don't take risks. If you're looking long-term, you're allowed to take risks.

Living on Less

Pre-retirement is sitting down and pretty much getting an idea of what it is you want to do with certain plans. All the while, in the back of your mind, knowing it means you're setting up a system for yourself where you're living on less.

I tell people if you make $100,000 and you spend $100,000, you're never going to be able to retire and keep the same lifestyle. In retirement, your pension (if you have one), plus your social security, may not equal $100,000 to maintain your current lifestyle. Altogether, they might equal something more like $60,000. That means there's a $40,000 shortage. That's simple math.

You're never going to be able to retire and maintain the same lifestyle—unless you build your lifestyle on living on less.

One possible strategy is to start living on less early, so if you make $100,000, you should live on $80,000 and stack that money for later on. If you're putting $20,000 away each year and living on $80,000 throughout, then you'll have $80,000 throughout retirement. You'll be accustomed to living on that lower budget, and when it comes time to retire, you can live on the same budget.

You want to create consistency so that retirement will be the same as if you were still working.

I always want to empower the person to be able to dictate what they do, so what I ask is, "Do you want to work in your retirement?" The term is work-optional retirement. It's financial independence. You have the power to retire and not have to work anymore, but you have the option. Better that you have the option than have it dictated to you.

People say that when they retire, they want to pay less in taxes. Your goal should be to pay the same amount of taxes because that means you maintain the same lifestyle.

I point out to my clients that if their boss came in and told them that they were able to avoid layoffs, but now instead of paying them $100,000, they will only pay them $90,000, they might be unhappy. But is that going to make them change jobs? Probably not. Well then, why aren't they putting that $10,000 away now?

You can do it, just try it. You're not really going to feel it. Just try it. If it doesn't work, scale it back. I tell people, right from the beginning, "I'm going to trick you into saving."

I'm Going to Trick You into Saving

Saving is a habit. It's hard to start, and it's hard to stop. Especially once you see your statements and realize your money is growing.

People find a way, especially when they understand the tax savings, to follow the plan. And then I explain how those savings affects the age of retirement.

When I ask my clients if it's going to be better to retire at age 55-65 or 65-75, the majority are going to say 55—and they should. Statistically speaking, they are going to be healthier, they'll remember things better, and it'll be easier to plan the trips they want to take.

We plan for a goal of 60, but we're going to try for 55. The worst-case scenario, if we can't quite make it to the 55, is at least we knew we were planning for 60.

We can put any ages in there, but if you're not planning for retirement, the is less of a chance of it happening.

Creating a habit of saving is very important. Money begets money. If they had $100,000 put away, and it generated 10 percent, it's much different than if they had $10,000 put away, and it generated 10 percent. In the beginning, putting money away is much more important than the actual return.

I remember a while ago I had a couple who were about 80 years old and had retired. I was sending them money, and the wife tells me very proudly, "I've been saving money."

"Where are you saving money?"

"Well, you send me the money, and I put it in the bank."

Inside, I'm thinking, that makes no sense! When you put it in the bank, it's not making any money for you. Why are they having me take it out of where it is making money just to put it in the bank?

"What's going on?"

She explains that she wants to go on trips. Her husband doesn't really like to travel but says he will, eventually, when he's 85!

"Listen," I told him, "You know where your health is right now. At age 85, we don't know if you're going to be in good health and I have a hard time believing that at age 85, you're going to look back and regret that you went on a cruise. I want you to do is do *something* by the next time I talk to you."

They went on a cruise, had a great time, and now they're going to take more cruises.

Sometimes people need an outside perspective to understand their situation.

I have another client who had retired and came in to tell me how upset he was about his grown children. They were living in his house, and he was worried about his finances.

I told my kids, "Listen, I'm not going to give up my retirement. I don't want my dreams to be squashed by you!"

He was so mad at them. I remember thinking that I wasn't sure why he was so worried and angry.

"What is it that you wanted to do?" I asked him.

There was a place in Florida that he had seen and had his heart set on.

"It would be like living the dream." he said. "But it would cost $6,000 a month."

"You're 70 right now. When do you think you would do that?"

"I don't know if I would ever do that. I'd have to sell this place."

"You gave your kids ultimatums about what to do, but the reality is, you're not touching any of the money you have with me," I told him. "What I'll tell you is that you can't take it with you. Let's start from there."

"You're already upset with your kids about helping them out now, so if you don't leave them a large inheritance it's not a big deal, right? Why don't you use some of that money?" I asked him. "Then, at 75, you can look back and say, 'I don't want to do this anymore' and move. I won't tell you that your kids are holding you up and you can't have your dream—it's on you. You *can* do it. I'm telling you; you can do it. And you know what? I *want* you to do it. Hurry up. Go look at that dream place because if you wait until you're 75, who knows where your health will be at that time?"

He ended up pursuing his dream, but on a smaller scale. He told me that after thinking about it and talking about it with his wife, there were things that they didn't need and they could get a smaller home.

I came to that same realization when I separated from my wife. At first, I was going to pursue all the different things we had together. I was going to get the same sort of house, a pool, a place with a nice lawn. Then it hit me as if someone was talking straight to me.

"What are you doing? Why are you trying to repeat exactly what went wrong before?"

I didn't need that much space for just myself. I didn't need a huge lawn or a pool. Was I going to mow that lawn or maintain that pool?

So, I moved into a nice townhouse that fits my needs. I don't mow the lawn. I don't shovel snow. I have a garage. I don't clean the pool. You reassess what you need as you live through life. You need to decide on your dream, make a realistic plan, and do it.

My client was blaming the fact that he wasn't living his dream on others when in truth, it was his inaction. He was waiting for something to happen.

That is where we lose control, when we wait for someone else's action before we do something. I know how frustrating it can be, and sometimes it's unavoidable, but a lot of times, it's not. Like the story about my clients who purchased the home in South Carolina—you don't always have to wait for it (Although, if the mortgage rate had been at 29 percent, I might have told them that the timing wasn't right.)

I remember talking to a very frustrated client late on a Thursday night.

"Man, I hate this job. I don't think I'll ever retire."

"What's going on?"

His wife was a teacher who had retired the previous year, and he wasn't enjoying his job.

So, I started going through the numbers. They were saving, putting in the maximum and living on less. She was receiving a pension. He did not intend to work once he retired.

"What you're working for right now is an extra $11,000 a year. That's probably easy to makeup, and you can probably spend less when you retire."

They left, and I didn't hear from them. Then I was in the store one day, and I bumped into them.

"Hey! How are you doing? What happened? Did you consider what I talked with you about?"

"Yeah," he said. "I went to work the next day, and something happened, so I said, 'I don't need this!' and I quit."

"Why didn't you tell me?!"

Retirement made all the sense in the world to him at that moment. I just spoke with him recently. He's been retired for about two years now. Sometimes you don't know that you can—and you need a little guidance from your financial advisor to make a change.

Some clients need a little more encouragement than others. I've had many clients where I would try to start that conversation—several times. One client made me prove that he could retire, seven different times, before he actually did it.

"When do you want to retire?"

"Oh, when I'm 65, seven years from now."

"What if I told you that you can stop working now?"

"Oh, I can't do that."

People are worried about how much money they will have in their retirement and if it will be enough. I can prove it over and over to them, but mentally speaking, sometimes people aren't ready for it.

So, they leave my office, but the thought is there in the back of their minds. The next time they start thinking, "Really? Could I stop working now? Maybe I should start thinking about that, but I don't want to retire yet. I want to make it to 62."

Each time they consider retirement, it changes a little bit, until finally, they come in with their minds made up.

"You know what? I'm done. What do we need to do?"

Sometimes it's difficult for my clients to stop working. They've devoted a large portion of their lives to their careers, their companies, their co-workers. There are a lot of emotions that come into play.

What will happen to them without me? What am I going to do? What's my purpose?

They can always find something to do, a purpose that is more identifiable to themselves than working, depending on their value system.

Financial independence, or what many call retirement, is an attainable dream with the right planning. It will look different depending on who you are. Find your goal and start the planning process as early as possible—your dream may come true.

PART THREE

And now what?

CHAPTER SEVEN

Parents

"Plan for the unexpected."

We all need to make sure that we are planning not just for ourselves, but also for our parents. Today, parents are living longer and will need care in their later years. When they pass, in addition to that loss, you will need to handle the financial aftermath and their legacy.

Role Reversal

We're in the sandwich generation. Not only are children living with their parents as adults, but parents are moving in too.

A few years ago, my parents were living with my sister in North Carolina. I had to go pick them up as they were going to be moving here to New York. We were trying to keep them out of a nursing home for as long as possible. So, I flew down, and I was driving back.

It was supposed to be a 10-hour drive from North Carolina to here. That day, it took thirteen.

I planned to take one, five-minute pit stop. Go to the bathroom, get a quick dinner, and get on the road. But as I'm taking my father in, he does this shuffle-walk that doesn't seem to be getting him anywhere, and my mom stops me as I'm trying to go in the store.

"Let me open the door for you," she said, her hand slowly reaching for the handle to the door.

I ended up stopping twice. The second stop, we used the bathroom, and I grabbed chips and water.

"This is what's for dinner," I told them. Then it was right back in the car.

So now it's dark, and my father is suffering from dementia. He's in the back seat, I'm driving, and my mom's in the front passenger seat. My father tells me in Spanish to turn on the lights.

"What do you mean, turn the lights on? What are you doing back there?"

"I'm looking for the keys."

"You're looking for the keys?"

Now, remember, I call him my father, but he's my uncle, and he's going to be living with my birth father now. He's looking for the keys to his house.

"We don't have those," I tell him.

"Oh. OK."

I turn off the lights, and it's quiet until again, I hear him tell me in Spanish to turn on the lights.

"What are you doing?"

"I'm looking for the keys."

He repeated this request about five or six times until finally, I get an idea.

"Turn on the lights!"

"What are you looking for, Dad?"

"I'm looking for the keys."

"Oh, I found them. They're in my pocket."

"Oh, OK."

A minute later, "Turn on the lights!"

Now my mom is getting fed up.

"He's trying to drive us home! Stop bothering him! He can't drive with the lights on! It's dark out!"

I turn out the lights. They turn on again.

"What are you doing?" my mom yells.

Now, remember, my father has dementia, and my mother is getting older. When it's dark outside, and the lights are on in the car, you see reflections in the windows.

"What are you doing? Pepe, get back in the car!"

"What are you talking about, Mom?"

My mom gestures out the window.

"What is he doing out there?"

"He's not outside of the car, Mom! We're driving 80 miles an hour on the Jersey Turnpike!"

Meanwhile, I'm driving, trying to watch the traffic and thinking, "Oh no, this was the one I didn't have to worry about!"

It's comical when you read it, but it's sad when you think about what happens, and what can happen with things like dementia. No one understands it until they see it and experience it. If you don't plan well, it can also have devastating effects financially.

When you see warning signs, make sure your parents have done their planning.

I would hear stories in the past about people and their parents. I remember first hearing about it around the turn of the millennium. I kept hearing more about parents and long-term care, but when someone told a story, I couldn't really relate to it. No one truly understands it until they see it and experience it.

Now, when I see someone like that, I can understand and relate. You can only laugh about these family stories. You take it with a grain of salt and a little bit of a laugher, but these stories are heartbreaking and emotionally draining to live through. My father passed a few years ago. My mom is still here, and she has her stories too.

It's a role reversal. You have to be aware of it, which is why I bring it up. Not only are you worrying about the people that are retiring now, or getting close to it, but we're the first generation that has to start worrying about the fact that people are living longer.

The odds are pretty good that you'll have a parent live to the age of 85 and need to move in with you.

The Social Security Administration has said that thanks to the Baby Boomer generation, 10,000 people will turn 65 every day until the 2030s. That's enough people to fill a major sports stadium every week.

Soon, there will be a flood of asset transfers. Without proper planning, there will also be a lot of headaches. You want to make sure that you have correctly executed tax strategies and paperwork.

When it comes to parents, Medicaid planning, long-term care, or nursing home planning is essential. If you don't do it first, it becomes not necessarily how much you can make, but how much you can keep and retain. You are going to spend a lot on nursing homes if you don't plan properly, in-advance.

It's an awkward, but unavoidable, conversation. You have to make sure that all the paperwork is in place to ensure that parents are cared for as they age. And, at the same time, we want their legacy to transfer in the way, and to whom, they desire. If the estate is incorrectly designed or executed, assets can be forfeited, resulting in parents receiving lesser care, with a smaller estate to pass on. There are things we can do to prepare.

I had that conversation with my parents, and we took care of the planning a long time ago. Not that it was easy. It didn't come without a little bit of encouragement *because* I'm their son; I'm still their little boy. Even though I'm a financial advisor, it is still hard for parents to take advice from their children.

Don't forget, however, that you have a generation coming up behind you. Are your children moving out, did they get a job, or are they moving in because they can't be on their own? We're the first generation that is worrying so much about their parents moving in and their children not moving out.

That's weird to think about, but there's bound to be a financial strain. Without the additional help of planning, a lot of money can get lost in the shuffle.

For some, their parents may pass away quickly. With my uncle we did the planning a long time ago and talked about a nursing home. As we started doing the planning for Medicaid to get an aide for him, he suddenly passed.

Then you have other stories where a parent is mentally there, but physically isn't doing well. Those parents are going to be around for another dozen years, not able to help themselves. There's a lot of assistance that's going to be needed. That is quite honestly, mentally exhausting too.

Without planning ahead of time, how are those issues going to be handled? That goes back to the first stage at the very beginning—make sure you have your stuff in order, right from the get-go. Stay that way, keep it consistent.

My biological father was awful at financial planning. He still is to this day. He has a great heart and wants to help others, but that sometimes translates into poor financial decisions.

Sometimes the household is like international relations. For example, we have America, with the branches of government as a kind of spousal relationship. The other countries around the world are relatives that need help from time to time. They come along like an uncle or a cousin, saying, "I need to borrow something." As America, we try to help as many of our relatives as we can.

After a while, you have to stop and think, "What am I doing?" Your generosity resulted in problems in your household budget. You need to pay medical bills or pay for a new roof or vehicle, but your finances are scattered among your relatives.

You must take care of your responsibilities first.

Understandably, you want to help your relatives and feel regret if you don't support them when they face a tough situation. Your home is like a microcosm of world finance. You must consider who you help and make sure you take care of yourself.

As a parent, you balance your budget and your desire to give your kids the world. As a grandparent, you have to realize that you can't shower your grandchildren with gifts if you can't afford it.

Sometimes as our parents get older, it's hard to get them to change those habits and patterns they have followed for longer than you have been alive—but it's not necessarily impossible.

Loss

Losing a parent is hard at any age, even without taking into account all of the financial implications.

My birth mother passed away in 2009. This past summer, for whatever reason, I desperately wanted to talk to her. I wanted to hear her voice. I had so many things to tell her about my life. I'm not sure what it was, but I just needed her.

It's funny how during different seasons, there's something that will trigger a flood of memories of someone that is gone. It could be a holiday, a favorite meal, or a scent that hurtles you back through time. I think anyone that has lost someone would agree.

There's always that one song on the radio that brings tears or laughter—and the memory of that person comes just a little closer.

For me at Christmas, it's the sound of children singing "Away in the Manger." When they sing it, I start to cry. My mother passed away on December 9, 2009, and it was playing when it happened—when I lost her.

You think about all of those family traditions that will never be the same again, that empty seat at the table, and the new traditions that will be born in their place.

It's something I often hear from my clients: "We did this at Thanksgiving and on Christmas we did this—and now they're not here."

For my family, it was hard, but it started a new tradition. Before my mom's passing, my brothers and sisters began gathering every April in Texas. I did not go for about four years.

"Why don't you go?" my sister kept asking me.

Sometimes you put off doing things, thinking you're going to do it later, and later never comes. It's almost like setting your life goals.

I've taken a new lease on life and decided to do more traveling now. I don't wait anymore for certain things. Goals are super-important, and if I want to do something, I put a schedule together and figure out the things I need to do to make it happen.

You take it step-by-step. You make a checklist and start working your way through it, and soon you'll discover that you accomplished much more than you would have otherwise. Everything just gets done somehow.

I have a running joke in my office about this. Back when Eileen, my assistant, first started working for me, she would be in a mild panic when she was trying to put together my schedule.

"What are we going to do, Robert? We have three appointments all coming in at the same time, and there's only one conference room available!"

"Relax," I told her. "It doesn't matter, just let it go and it all kind of works out in the end."

Somehow, it always did. That was six years ago, and now we've hired a new person to do the scheduling.

"Oh, no! We have two people—!"

"What do you tell her, Eileen?" I asked.

"Robert says it always works out," said Eileen. "And it always does."

It's the most bizarre thing. It's a piece of wisdom I picked up from a little movie called "Shakespeare in Love."

Legacy

I remember the first wake I ever attended. I had been very hesitant to go. I didn't know the person who had passed. Someone pointed out that the wake isn't for the person who has gone—it's for those that are still here.

The same is true of preparing for the final transfer of assets. Parents want to make sure that their legacy passes on the way they envision, with as little difficulty as possible for their loved ones.

There is a legacy for those left behind, but without proper planning, the transfer can be a bumpy road.

When my father (my uncle) passed last year, it was clear that the estate was not as organized as I was hoping. I'm still working on it, trying to find the time to take care of certain things. Along the way, my parents had lost their birth certificates, their marriage certificate, her driver's license, and social security card.

As I try to handle different situations, I'm sent off from one place to other because of the missing documents. Because I don't have her license, I have to go over here and get this. Because we don't have their marriage license, I have to find a way to prove that they're married.

Despite what people may tell you, "common law marriage" is most definitely not a legal thing and does not exist. I'd never thought much of it because my parents did get married, but now the marriage license is lost, as are some of my mother's memories.

Now, this is the same person that told me we went to Disney World.

"We got married, oh, I think it was a few years ago."

"What do you mean it was a few years ago? You were down in North Carolina."

"Oh. Well then, maybe it was in the seventies."

She couldn't remember where they were married either. It took me five months to find the certificate. I finally enlisted my sister in the search, and we went to Ellenville, one of the places where my mother thought they might have been married.

We had them check from the 1970s to the 1990s. No luck.

We tried to search online, but to access the records, you have to provide a driver's license number. Great.

Finally, my sister came through. She found it in Monticello.

"Why did you go to Monticello?" I asked my mom, flabbergasted.

At any rate, I had gathered all of the paperwork I needed for the visit to the Social Security office, and I went in, all proud of myself.

"We need her social security card—and, where is she? We don't accept the power of attorney."

I'm a financial advisor, and this was a revelation to me. A power of attorney works everywhere else, but not at Social Security.

We're still working on getting my father's Social Security payments sent to my mother.

I really could write a book just entirely about my parents.

My parents aren't the only ones doing life their way. I remember one instance where the couple lived on a family estate where there were multiple houses on the property. When they passed, we found out they were a bit old school. Their family members went through the house and found money stashed in books and various other locations all over the place. That's just the way they did things in the past.

Make Preparations

Sometimes parents need encouragement to start getting their estate in order. The important thing, however, is to have them do it early before they can't remember, or something happens.

I remember having a conversation about this with the children of one of my clients.

"I've been talking to your father. Do you notice anything different in your conversations with him?" I had noticed a change in him at our recent meeting. He had always struck me as being as smart as a whip.

"No," they told me, then after a moment, "Well, sometimes he repeats things. He gets kind of annoying."

This is a warning sign to make sure that everything is in order. Not necessarily that your parent is going to pass soon, but their decision-making skills are deteriorating.

Our decision making is more likely to be better in our early fifties than in our late seventies.

If you have a parent that is 75, they may be stuck in their ways, but you have to guide them to someone that you both can trust. Then things can be done right, so there isn't a burden to the surviving family.

In this case, I worked quickly with his lawyers to handle his real estate investments, prepare trusts, and make sure that everything would transfer without probate.

At this point, if something were to happen to him, it would be a phone call and a couple of weeks of work. Everything is handled. The family can enjoy their time without worrying about the financial side of things. If we don't prepare properly, there is more work and stress later on.

Part of making the preparations is making sure that the children, or whoever is going to handle matters, know what to do when the parent passes.

There have been phone conversations with grieving family members, asking harried questions: "Oh my gosh, how do we pay this bill? Where did they put this? How did he file this? How did she do this? What goes on over here? How are we supposed to get this? Who is supposed to take care of that?"

Life is not in order, and the loved ones are overwhelmed, not just with understandable grief, but also with stress over financial concerns. It's such a big ordeal for them. It can be avoided simply by doing a little planning ahead of time—and passing on that information.

Whoever is going to be handling the transfer of the assets should have access to the information, not be left in the dark. They should know the name of the attorney or the insurance company, and whether the parent wants to be buried or cremated.

Clients can bring their child or the person who is going to handle the estate to meet with me, but I always ask them exactly what they want to disclose. Their child doesn't necessarily need to know how much money the parents have. However, someone needs to know what is going to happen in the event of the client's passing and that they can call me if something should occur.

Long before my father passed, we spoke about what he wanted to happen after he was gone.

"If I pass, make sure you don't cremate me." my father said.

I remember it so vividly, even though it was decades ago because I remember asking him if he was sure that was what he wanted.

When he did pass, we were making funeral arrangements, and at the last minute, my mom says, "I think he wanted to be cremated."

"No, Mom, you want to be cremated. He wanted to be buried."

He had said it all his life, right up until he passed. I had written it down for him. Afterward, I thought about it. Imagine if I didn't have that conversation with him, or if I didn't write it down. What would have happened? His wishes wouldn't have been followed.

Fading memories and the stressful situation can cause someone's final wishes to go unfulfilled. The best thing to do is to have everything planned and written down in advance. You don't want to think about it at that time.

Just recently, I had a client pass away. His planning was completely finished and meticulous. His legacy was taken care of in only one month. Not every estate will be finished in a month, and situations may arise that are more complicated. However, without planning, usually, it takes about a year or so.

The amount of time depends on the types of assets. There are so many vehicles to utilize that I'm not even mentioning some of the things that can be done. I try to keep things as simple as possible, so it's not as intimidating. Even with that said, many different tools can be utilized to assist with an estate. Most people don't even know the tools exist—or if they do, they don't understand how using those tools pertain to them or, if a specific tool works for their situation.

Get the Right Attorney

When the time comes, make sure you hire the right kind of attorney.

One of my clients passed, and his surviving family wanted to work with the long-time family attorney who did not specialize in estate planning. Financial planning was just not in his realm of expertise.

This is equivalent to a doctor specializing in gastrointestinal issues taking on a patient with an eye issue. They're just not equipped to help you.

He ended up convoluting the whole estate. In this particular situation, there were four children and then a step-child, not blood-related. Things just got haywire in the end. Because of the estate design, contrary to the wishes of the parent, the step-child received nothing. There may have been strategies to incorporate this child into the estate. But now, this child was entirely pushed away. It was awful.

It turned out to be a situation where someone was meddling where they probably shouldn't have.

The takeaway from this is that you need a trusted estate attorney. Get the right attorney for the right situation.

In the end, they brought in a knowledgeable attorney and got things cleared up, but what had happened to the step-child was not reversible. While we knew that my client wanted the step-child to get something, it turned out that after all the fighting and attorney's fees, the child didn't get anything.

It was sad to see and know that it was a combination of an attorney not in his area of knowledge and the fact that money makes people crazy.

"You know, Robert, you'll see that when it comes to money, money makes people act funny."

It was a straightforward but valuable lesson from my uncle many years ago. It has been proven true over and over again throughout my career.

As I'm talking to different families when a client passes, sometimes other people start coming out of the woodwork. You've never heard of them and then suddenly you get these calls. Ultimately, they want to ask if they are inheriting anything.

One person almost always wants to inherit more than the others. Sometimes there is a story about the families past used as an excuse for bad behavior! You don't want to hear about that!

Other times it's the controlling personalities that appear before the client passes. I just found out recently that one of my family members is very controlling of an elderly family member and doesn't let her talk to people. If you want to talk to her, you have to go through the controller.

In these scenarios, older adults can be intimidated into signing things over because they have been isolated and are, essentially, being held, hostage.

Money makes people do crazy things.

Fortunately, I have also seen the polar opposite during my career. There have been several families that came in and said, "Whatever takes care of mom, that's fine."

I love to hear that.

I had another client decide that she wanted to go to a retirement community. When her children and I examined her estate, we found that she'd be able to do that and still have money to do all the different things she wanted to do. She was thrilled. It was the impact of planning that made her dream possible.

She was so happy that she could move into the retirement community and still have money to do all the different things she wanted to do.

I have also had clients that decided to pass on their legacy while they were still alive. It makes sense if you don't need it. You can pass it on and watch your family enjoy a trip to Disney World or whatever it might be.

Visit Often

It's essential to come in periodically and take a look at everything, especially when a big event happens like a trip to the hospital. There's always something missed or forgotten along the way.

There was this one instance where dividends were still coming into the estate. The client had passed. She had forgotten about some of her stocks, and the family didn't know about it either. People forget things. It happens. If you come in for a financial check-up periodically, many of these things can be caught ahead of time.

When we do the review, I look to find out if you need anything else, if you need more money from your assets, and how everything is going. I always want to learn more about my clients. When I talk to them, I get to know more about them, not just about their money. I also want to know what is going on in their lives and what they like to do. That's the driver of financial planning.

"What do you want to do?"

"I just want to enjoy the rest of my life."

"Well, what do you enjoy?"

They tell you all the different things they like to do, and you get to know them a little more each time, not just as clients, but as people.

That's why I say I probably will never retire. I enjoy talking to people too much.

CHAPTER EIGHT

Loss of Spouse

I had one client who kept putting off retirement, even though I told him that he could stop working. He didn't want to retire until he was 65. Finally, he said, "OK, let's do it in one year." The year came and went, and he still worked another couple of years. Finally, he retired three years "early" for him, at age 62.

He welcomed two grandchildren, then a third. Then, three years after he had retired, he went into surgery and didn't come out. It was tough, but imagine if he didn't have that personal time with his family? What if he had just worked until he went into surgery and never got to enjoy that retirement with his family?

It is crucial to note that he planned for his wife in case of just this situation. You can never replace a person, but you can make it so that their family doesn't have to worry and can go on trying to live a fulfilled life.

Looking out for your Family

It's a tough subject to think about, but you don't want your family to be stressed about financial issues later. There are certain realities. Everybody is going to die. How are you going to make sure that everything is done the way you want it to happen?

I remember a conversation with my birth mother a couple of years before she passed. She was explaining to me how she worries about each of her ten kids. I'm her youngest.

"That's a lot of worries to have, Mom."

"With each of you I worry in different ways."

"Well Mom, don't worry about me, I'm doing fine. So, take it off your shoulders and don't worry about me."

"I can't. You're my child. I'm always going to worry about you."

I was thinking about that short conversation afterward. I only have two daughters, but I get it. It doesn't matter their ages, maybe it compounds with more children, but the worry is still there, regardless of their regardless of what they're doing. At any point in time, something can happen.

I had a client who was married, with four older children. While we were doing the planning, he passed away. His wife started getting dementia, and then before she died, one of the sons died. These things can happen. And yes, it foils a plan to a certain extent, but it can still be addressed if you do things thoroughly so that everything will be worked out for the surviving family.

I always want to make sure that we protect them in case something unfavorable happens.

People start their careers, go out into the world and start to accomplish their goals. They become so busy with success and life that they never have time to consider what will happen when they pass. Now they're 70 years old, and they have different properties, a will, and other estate issues. They need to get everything wrapped up, and tell their loved ones what is supposed to happen. That way, when a spouse passes, the surviving spouse doesn't have to worry about anything.

That is the way it should be. The surviving family should be free to tackle the issues of the heart because the financial hurdles are already settled.

The unavoidable thought should be, "How are we going to do Thanksgiving this year? How are we going to do Christmas? Who is going to be sitting next to me when I go somewhere? If I'm feeling lonely, who do I lean on?"

The concern shouldn't be, "How am I going to pay my bills?"

What do I do without my spouse?

Losing a spouse can happen at any age. I recently had a client pass away after seeing him just two weeks before. He was 87 years old, but he was active, running 5k races, and driving from New Jersey to meet with me. The last time I saw him, he made an appointment to meet with me again in the next quarter.

Then I received the call that he had passed, and his wife met with me. The conversations with him were always focused on ensuring that his wife could take care of herself if something were to happen to him. Everything had been well planned.

We reminisced about him, and she spoke about how life had changed, like the mice.

"What do you mean?" I asked.

She explained that he always set up the mousetraps in the basement and took care of "those kinds" of things—it was his job. Now, "little things" like dead rodents in the cellar shine a light on her loss. Recently, she had to face them without him.

"My daughter and I went downstairs. We had gloves and masks on, and we screamed, 'Oh my God!' the whole time. But they had to be taken care of." she said.

The empty place setting at the dinner table. The mousetraps in the basement. The whiff of a particular brand of perfume. These are the things that people don't think about until that person is missing from their lives. The same is sometimes true on the financial side unless there is proper planning. Dealing with mousetraps isn't as overwhelming when the financial plan is in order.

The common recurring theme among my married clients is a concern that the surviving spouse will be able to take care of themselves. It's not that either is expected to pass soon, but the reality is that eventually, it will happen.

Sometimes when it does, the surviving spouse realizes they didn't know anything about the finances. I remember one client who came in after her husband passed away. She was in her early to mid-fifties, and she was distraught.

She came in and told me that she didn't know what to do. Her husband used to do everything. Their children were grown up, out of school, out of college, and she wasn't sure what to do next.

"I'm beside myself, and I've got this house," she said.

As a financial advisor, you have to have some realistic conversations, especially if you're meeting the client for the first time and they never did planning before. He had an appropriate amount of life insurance.

One of the questions that has to be asked is, "Does it makes sense for the surviving spouse to move?" It can be a hard question as there are emotions attached to the decision. People don't want to leave their homes. It's not because of the house itself. Instead, leaving the house represents leaving the many memories that live in each one of the rooms.

It's basically about getting the house in order. Then there are different things to deal with, whether it's the loneliness, or making sure their family will be OK. The client can then be confident that their advisor can help in this highly stressful situation.

The conversation was almost like therapy for her.

"You can do this. You have to try. Come back next time and tell me about your progress."

She ended up getting a job and became a strong leader in real estate. She was able to make enough money so as not to worry about tapping into the money she had. Sometimes my job entails empowering people to feel that they are capable of making their way. She was always capable. I just pointed that out to her and encouraged her.

CHAPTER NINE

The Journey goes on

"...and you can't take it with you."

We've all heard the saying before that life is short. Life can be fun. We should enjoy it. We're not going to live forever.

If I haven't made it clear, when I say your journey goes on, it is a metaphor. The journey is your estate. Live and love life and care about the ones that are with you, while they're with you. I think that's important.

The other part of that metaphor is that your journey—your estate—goes on, and you can't take it with you. When you pass away, it's going to go to somebody. The question is whether you want it to pass conveniently to your heirs.

If you pass away and nothing is prepared, all of the burdens fall on your loved ones. Now they have to deal with everything that an estate entails, while mourning their loss.

Almost every parent says they want their children to live a better life than they lived. That's why we make sure we plan so that we can preserve what we've worked so hard to earn over our lifetime and pass it along to them with minimal dissipation or tax loss.

If I could give my clients advice before they walked through my door, it would be to adopt saving as a habit. It's always going to help you.

In the beginning, it's putting it in for later. Later on, it's just having more accumulated for emergency needs. In retirement, it's because you had that habit of saving that you'll be able to attain financial independence earlier. Some will even find that if they were good savers, they're still saving even in retirement.

As with almost anything else in life, sometimes people go to the extreme, worrying about saving and forgetting to enjoy what they have. I don't want you to go overboard, and all you do is save money, never taking the time to enjoy the people and possibilities in your life.

So, don't take life too seriously and don't be a maniac about saving.

We do only live once.

I've found that it is rare for someone on their deathbed to voice regrets over that cruise they took, or the family vacation that created the fond memories that your loved ones will cherish when you're gone. That doesn't happen.

This book has taken you on a journey through most of the major turning points of an average life. The stories I've shared are from situations that have happened over the course of my career as a financial advisor.

There are other situations that can and will happen but may not be covered in this book. Those can be addressed in a more personal setting. Each case should be treated individually. As much as things are the same, they are different.

Sometimes, what seems like a major problem for one person is not so problematic for another person.

The reality is that the majority of people if they had guidance, to begin with, wouldn't walk into my office with a significant financial burden. When we start to talk and plan, they realize that they have lost valuable time, which may have been useful for a better retirement outcome.

In some situations, they walk in not necessarily with a problem but having made a choice that I would have counseled them to have made a little differently.

It's good to have a third-party walking through important life decisions with you. It's sort of like your primary care physician. They can go over your current health, potential warning signs, and make recommendations to make your life better and longer.

But the doctor—and your financial advisor—can't force you to follow the recommendations and take your medicine. That is your responsibility.

You will be in any one of the stages covered in this book during your life. This book may give you some helpful direction, but it is best to sit down with a financial advisor to make sure that you and your family are financially sound.

You could do your financial planning on your own, but if you work with an advisor, you will benefit from their expertise and save yourself some anxiety. To make sound decisions, you need to have knowledge of the financial markets, the time to do it, and the desire to want to do it. If you don't have the luxury of all three things, you shouldn't be doing it on your own.

However, if you do, by all means, you should. That's fine, too. But the reason I'm in business is that the majority of people don't have all three. You need a trained advisor that can give your dream the attention it deserves.

In an ever-changing environment, I continue to attend seminars to keep current. I speak with other advisors around the country to learn what they've come across and to exchange stories. I hold local seminars and speak on various topics from real estate to social security to advice for teachers. This is what I love to do, and I do it every day.

When you become a client of Quest Financial Services, you will have a financial plan that is tailored to your specific life stage, needs, and dreams. We would be honored to work with you as your guide on your financial quest.

AUTHOR BIO

Robert Cepeda, CFP is the co-founder, managing partner and senior wealth advisor for Quest Financial Services. For more than 25 years he has continuously sharpened the art of listening. He invites you to join in a conversation that focuses directly on you. It has been the foundation of his practice from the early nineties and remains the cornerstone of his work as a Certified Financial Planner in New York's Hudson Valley region.

He is also a seasoned public speaker, having developed and delivered educational programs such as "Rebuild Your Life After Loss," "Women and Investing" and "Get Your Financial House in Order." These events provide a comfortable forum for expression, encouragement and inspiration.

Robert is a graduate of the University of Rochester, with a degree in Economics and Certificate of Management in Accounting and Finance. He holds a series 24, 7, and 63.

Made in the USA
Monee, IL
26 August 2019